Senior Cat Care

How To Take Care of Your Elderly Cat

From the View of a Cat

Tomsyn

Copyright 2015 – J I & T Treasures

Dedication

I want to dedicate this book to four exceptionally remarkable people in my life.

My mother and father, Iris and Jerry, who have always been there for me, and believed in me no matter what. They have always stood by my side, giving me encouragement all the way. They always encouraged me to explore my creative side. Even when my first attempts were not always precise, they knew how to give criticism in a warm and positive way. My parents always knew how to bring out the good in me.

My godmother and godfather, Karen and Bob, who are the world's greatest godparents a godson could ever ask for. They always stood by my side and gave me inspiration. When I would sometimes come up with some weird ideas, they would still support me. My godparents have always been there for me, no matter what.

I was blessed with four incredible parents, whom I love very much and hold dearly in my heart. They are my world, and always will be now and forever.

Love you all.

I would also love to dedicate this book to our great pets. My parents always believe that having pets in our lives, make us a better person.

A Special dedication for FoxFace, who inspired this book, and who died a month after this eBook was written in my mother's arms. She died at the age of 20, which is 98 in human years.

Acknowledgment

I would like to give out a special thank you to my Mom Iris for proof reading and editing this book. A special thank you to Dorothy K. who is a dear friend, who also had proof read and edited this book. Without these two great people, it would have taken longer in completing this book.

Special thanks go out to my friend Carol M., Craig T. and my many friends from work: Brenda D., Cindy S., Dorothy K., Elyse M., Eric S., Glenn S., Heather D., Jeff G., Jeff H., Michael D., Neina A., Robyn R., Sallie R., Scott D., Siobhan C., Sue A., and Trudy S. who all have been always supportive of me. These are great people and great friends.

To Dennis and Monica R, my neighbors, who are like family more than a neighbor.

A thank you to Hank N. for driving me to be successful in whatever path I take.

A special thank you to Glenn S., who always in his own Christian way, kept me grounded.

A Thank you to all animal lovers who have a heart to give these great four legged animals a home, making them part of their family.

Limits of Liability – Disclaimer of Warranty

This book contains material protected under International and Federal copyright laws and treaties. Any unauthorized reprint or use of this material is prohibited. No part of this book may be reproduced or transmitted in any form by any means, graphic, electronic, or mechanical, including photocopying, recording, taping, or by any information storage or retrieval system, without permission in writing from the publisher(s).

Warning and Disclaimer: The information offered in this book is offered with the understanding that it does not contain legal, financial, tax, or other professional advice. Individuals requiring such services should consult a competent professional. This material is provided "as is" without warranty of any kind. The author(s) and publisher(s) make no representation or warranties with respect to the accuracy, applicability, fitness, or completeness of the contents of this book or information. Information in this book may be updated at any time without notice. The author(s) and publisher(s) make no representations about the suitability of the information contained in the book for any purpose.

The author(s) and publisher(s) of this book have used best efforts in preparing this material. Although every effort has been made to ensure the accuracy of the contents of this book and accompanying material, errors and omissions can occur. The author(s) and publisher(s) assume no responsibility for any damages whatsoever arising from the use of this book and information, or alleged to have resulted in connection with this book or information. This book and information is not completely comprehensive. This book and information is offered only as an opinion of the author(s) and publisher(s). Some readers may wish to consult additional books or sources for advice.

Links and products referenced in the text are owned and operated by a third party. The author(s) and publisher(s) have no affiliation with these third party individuals, or firms and have no control over any information offered on sites or other media. Such links and references are included "as is" for reference purposes only.

Trademarks referred to in this book are the acknowledge property of the Trademark owners and are used for reference purposes only. Registered trademarks used within the text will not include registered markings. This book and accompanying information is not authorized or endorsed by Amazon, Barns & Noble, Microsoft, Adobe Systems or any other firm, company or individual mentioned in the text.

©2015. Tomsyn. All Rights Reserved. This material may not be reproduced in any manner whatsoever, in whole or in part, without express, written consent from the author. Violators will be prosecuted.

About: This Book

Senior Cat Care ... How to Take Care of Your Elderly Cat ... From the View of a Cat is written specifically for cat lovers who have elderly cats.

The target audience for this book are those who have elderly cats, and want the best they can give their love ones during their elderly age. This is a great guide for those who want to know what they should be doing for their elderly cat. Most owners treat their elderly cats as if they are still that young kitten they remember, this is not good for a senior cat.

This book was written in a unique way, that it was told through the eyes of a senior cat. This makes learning of taking care of an elderly cat even funnier due to the personality of my senior cat, FoxFace.

Taking care of an elderly cat the correct way, will help prolong their lives, and make their ending years more enjoyable, and less stressful. It is important to know the right things to do, so that your elderly cat is not being stressed out.

When we chose to bring that special cat into our lives, they become a part of our family. We owe them the best lives that we can give them. We owe them the best care when we get them as kittens, and as they age. The way you take care of a kitten, is way different when they become an elderly cat. This book will help you in knowing how to take care of your elderly cat, the right way, from the view of a cat.

I really hope you enjoy reading this book. If so, please leave our author a good rating and a great review. You are an integral part of our continued success. Please also share with your friends on Facebook and Twitter. Our number one goal is to help our four legged family members.

About: The Author

My whole life I have been around animals. My parents, specially my mother are a huge animal lover, and I guess that just rubbed off on me. There was not a time that I cannot remember when we did not have pets around our house.

We had horses, dogs, cats, rabbits, guinea pigs, turtles, chickens, geese and even birds. When my parents got a farm, my mother, a huge cat lover, had a trailer that she had used to help taken in stranded cats. We had 14 cats that we took care of and provided them with a great home. Of course we would have them spade so that they would not be able to reproduce; otherwise we would have too many cats. The trailer was set up great, heat in the winter, air conditioning in the summer.

Over the years, I have learned so much about these different animals. My mother, who was so smart, knew so much that we even had our own remedies in taking care of these cats. Of course our veterinarian helped with some of these also. This would be from cleaning, feeding and taking caring of them on all different levels.

So I felt that with my 45 years' experience working with these types of animals, and having our animals live into senior age, felt that I should write about how we did things to help others. All our pets lived past their normal ages, due to the way we had cared for them.

This is a cat series that I have written, based off of the Cat's Point of View. I think that you will enjoy it, because it comes from the view of the cat. It is a great humorous way of learning for all ages.

Forward

This book is for all cat lovers everywhere. Tomsyn did a great job, for cat lovers who have senior cats, who found that there really was not much out there to help in taking care of our four legged love ones.

The How to's of, "Taking Care of Elderly Cats, From the Cats Point a View." is an in depth and an eye opener for cat lovers. Tomsyn gives informative information from the cats' point of view, making this book funny. It allows an insight into the cat's world, and provides us with information that some of us cat owners did not know. You can feel FoxFace's temperaments and attitudes, which made this a great book to read.

Tomsyn covers from feeding, grooming to exercising your senior cat. These things are very important in helping your senior cat to live a healthy life as they age.

This is a must read for anyone that has a cat or plans to get one. This book is a useful tool no matter what age your cat is. It is truly a learning experience. I am looking forward to Tomsyn's other cats books that are soon coming out.

Dorothy Kramer

Contents

Dedication..2
Acknowledgment..4
Limits of Liability – Disclaimer of Warranty..6
   Warning and Disclaimer..6
About: This Book..9
About: The Author..11
Forward..13
Contents..14
Section 1 - Watering and Food...16
   WATER..16
   FOOD..21
Section 2 – Grooming..31
   Using Grooming as Bonding Time...31
   Grooming as a Health Check..34
   Brushing..37
      Basic equipment you need for grooming your cat...............38
      Basic brushing techniques on seniors...............................40
      Preventing Hairballs..43
      Getting knots and Matted hair out....................................44
      Trimming Your Cat's Hair..46
   Nails...47
      The basic tools for your cat's nails....................................47
      Basic care before you start trimming...............................47
      How to trim the nails correctly and safely.......................48
   Bathing..51
      Using the right shampoo..51
      Basic Things you Need...51

    Bathing 52
        How to Bath your Senior 53
    Ears 54
        Examine the Ear 55
        Cleaning the Ear 56
        Infected Ears 58
    Eyes 60
        Washing the Eye 60
        Checking our Eyes 61
    Cleaning the Teeth 63
    Nose 64
    When is a Professional Groomer Needed? 67

Section 3 – Exercising 68
    Exercising 69
    Having Play Time 70
    Toys 71
    Safety 73

Conclusion 75
A Thank you 76
Preview of Next Book in the Series – Vol. 2 77
Preview of Third Book in the Series – Vol. 3 79
Other Books by J I & T Treasures 81

Section 1 - Watering and Food

Meow, meow, meoooww, wait a minute – let me get this hair ball out so that I can speak your language and you can actually understand me. My name is FoxFace, or at least that is what my human owners call me. I am 98 years old, which is 20 in the human world. I overhear them say it is remarkable that I am still kicking, because most of us do not live this long. However, with the proper care and regular visits to our veterinarian, I can still live a long and healthy life. What made me wish to dedicate this book to my owner is that not too many humans know how to properly take care of us old senior cats.

Senior cats typically need more care and attention than younger cats. Even though we are independent and love our freedom of choice, we still need our human companions to help us, especially as we age.

WATER

Water is one of the most important things senior cats need, not only because we need it to keep our body functioning correctly but because our body weight is 60-70 percent water. Our wild cat relatives get most of their water from the prey they catch. Personally, I prefer to have my human bring me the food; why work hard for it, when it can just be served to me? In order to help us digest our food better as we age, water consumption is very important for us, as it is for you humans.

Sometimes, as we age, we like to eat wet food more because of the liquid content. However, my veterinarian tells my owner that it is still better to ensure that I drink more plain water. If you are serving dry food to your senior cat, please remember that plain water is even more necessary. I will discuss more about food later, which is my favorite topic.

Our humans always say that we are picky, but as we get older, that is not necessarily the case – we are just old and cranky. If you were 98 years old, you too would be a little cranky. Moving around is not as easy for me as it was in the good old days, when I was young and chased a ball or yarn and scooted around under the blanket while my human tried to make the bed. So, please bear with us senior cats; we need to be treated with care and lots of love.

So, what I have to say next is not meant to sound picky; it is just what we senior cats hate about our water. We are more sensitive to the taste of water and particularly dislike the chlorine taint that tap water has. If you must serve us tap water, let it settle for a while, or, better yet, let it sit in the refrigerator and get cold. This will make it taste a lot better for us. The best water that you could serve us, as my human does, is filtered water or mineral water. If you live in the country and your humans have a water softener, you should not serve us this water because of the salt content, which is not very healthy for us nor for any of your other animals. If you have decent, clean well water, that is better for us than water that passes through a water softener.

The other day, I was sitting on my human's lap, and she was reading about how plastic bottles and aluminum cans are not acceptable to drink out of and how some pop companies are planning to go back to using glass. Boy, I knew this a long time ago. (As if she thought I was listening to her...well, she doesn't have to know that I was.) Anyway, cats do not like the smell of plastic, which may be why your cats are not drinking their water. Our water should be served in a glass or ceramic, crock-type bowl, which does not give out any toxins or odors, making them safe for us and keeping the water cold longer.

As we senior cats get older, dehydration is an extremely serious concern, so you should try to place water bowls near our resting places as well as by our food. As we get older, it is sometimes difficult for us to move from one place to another, so having the water closer makes it easier to ensure we are getting enough to drink. Humans should also keep an eye on our water bowls; even though it is common for older cats to drink more water, drinking more dramatically in this manner can indicate kidney problems. As we get older, it is common for our kidneys to work less efficiently, so you need to keep an eye on us and our habits.

Cystitis is an inflammation of the bladder; it may precede or be secondary to urolithiasis (stones in the urinary tract). Cystitis causes discomfort, and you have to take us to the veterinarian. If your cat has kidney disease, he or she can be put on a prescription diet if you catch it early. Who knows, there may even be another reason that we start to drink more, so any unexplained increase of thirst should be investigated by our veterinarian.

In my younger days, I was always a thin, gorgeous feline. However, as we get older, we thin cats are more susceptible to dehydration because most of the body's water is stored in muscle, and our kidneys begin to lose the ability to conserve water. So, please keep an especially watchful eye on your thinner cats.

Now, personally, I love my wet food even though my veterinarian recommends dry foods. I love my wet food because it is easier to eat, and because I do not drink as much water as I should, wet food helps keep me from dehydrating. Now, if you do feed your cats dry food, and it is getting hard for them to chew, you can moisten it a little. Be careful not to add too much water – we hate eating mush.

As I mentioned, make sure you do keep fresh water around for us, because those of us that do not drink a sufficient amount of water are more susceptible to urinary tract crystal formation and, perhaps, kidney disease as well.

Now, my veterinarian mentioned that feeding us canned food or even fresh home-cooked diet foods will help avoid problems. However, if your cat is weak – not just lazy – try scattering multiple water dishes around the house. My veterinarian mentioned that sometimes a recirculating fountain or drippy faucet will draw our attention. I have to admit that this does draw my attention, but it does not necessarily make me want to drink. If the water has a terrible smell or foul taste, I would not care if it was a whole waterfall right in front of me. Another excellent idea is mixing canned and dry foods together so that the liquid of the canned food can be absorbed by the dry, making it moist.

FOOD

As we get older, our digestive system becomes less efficient, which requires us to eat several smaller meals rather than two or so larger meals. Just like you when you get older, you cannot eat the foods you once loved as you did. Our digestive system starts to work slower, and our metabolism has a harder time breaking down the nutrients and proteins. It is better to give your cat smaller and more regular meals throughout the day, but I think my owner's style works just fine for me. She leaves out the food for the entire day, and I eat whenever I want. It is degrading for us to have to beg each time we want to eat. Of course! If you have a cat that is large and, ultimately, in need of a diet, you should take away the food periodically. A well-balanced diet of wet and dry foods has all the vitamins and minerals that we need.

In this section, I want to talk about wet and dry foods. There are a variety of excellent senior cat food brands out there, and you can ask your veterinarian to recommend one that is right for your cat. Senior cats are prone to losing weight because of inconsistent eating habits. Sometimes, we eat less because we are simply disinterested in food. If you notice such tendencies, you should take your cat to the veterinarian. However, we might have a sudden increase in appetite but without weight gain, which should be investigated.

Besides weight loss, it is imperative that you watch for other signs of nutritional deficiency such as a thin, dull coat; extreme shedding; dandruff; weight loss; vomiting; queasiness; diarrhea; offensive breath; and yellow teeth. These are all warning signs that should not be ignored, for they indicate something is most likely wrong. The problem could be intestinal, dental, or something even more serious. Furthermore, if your cat wobbles as it walks; it is probably receiving too many calories for its level of activity and should either cut down on food intake or exercise more.

As we become less active, we do not need as much food. It is not advisable to overfeed us, for we gain weight and our old bodies cannot handle it. There are foods that are made for senior cats that have less protein and fat and more fiber; this lowers calories while still making us feel full. Some of us senior cats may actually get thinner because our digestive systems are weakening, as they have become less efficient at using the nutrients in our food.

In general, cats that are seven years old and older start taking life a little slower. Because of this, their nutritional needs start to change. We need a high-quality diet, one that would help us digest a good amount of protein, for protein becomes more critical than ever in order to help maintain our overall body condition.

Even though it is not acceptable for our health and figures, we felines thrive on foods that are high in moisture (canned or fresh). We prefer high levels of meat protein and fat content balanced with our essential minerals. The National Research Council formulates the commercial diets that we felines should be on. Most pet food manufacturers rely on this information, so all National brands are remarkably similar in their nutrient content. By nature, we do not thrive on carbohydrates or plant-derived proteins.

Do not buy the cheapest cat foods just because they are cheap. Price may proportionally correlate with health value. In most cases, the lower the price, the lower the quality of the ingredients. So please do not feed your cat generic or house brand cat foods. Normally, mid- or average-priced cat foods will have higher-quality ingredients. If you want to spoil your cat, most national brands have premium formulas that are a little better.

Most of us cats enjoy a variety of foods, including canned, semi-moist, and dry. On occasions, some of us even like cooked meats and fish. I myself love cooked chicken, ham, and even beef. Of course, they have to be warm to the touch to eat. Make sure that you are feeding your cats a complete cat food that provides a balanced diet. If you do feed your cat things like chicken, ham, or even beef, make sure that this is not a regular thing. I hate to say that because it tastes so delicious, but it is unsuitable for our digestion and health. Most veterinarians also recommend that if you do feed your cat canned food, whatever your cat does not eat should be put into the refrigerator so it will not become stale or attract flies, for these things can cause digestive upsets. If you would, please, also take the food out of the cans and put it into a ceramic crock pot or glass bowl; the tin of the cans is not acceptable for us either, for it can cause hyperthyroidism. Besides, those cans have sharp edges on them.

Our digestive system slows down as we get older, so you seriously must watch our diets closely. Sometimes, we might have health problems and need particular foods that are specially formulated for seniors. Some of these special foods are even tailored to our individual health conditions like diabetes, kidney and heart disease, and dental problems. Furthermore, make sure we do not put on too much weight because that puts a strain on our body systems. Hey, if you want us to stick around, you have to make sure our figures are slimmed. At the same time, you must make sure we do not lose weight rapidly either, as that can cause a more serious problem such as thyroid or kidney disease. If you see your feline starting to lose weight rapidly, have him checked out by his veterinarian.

My owners always check with my veterinarian to see what would be an appropriate diet for me; you should do the same for your feline. Each cat may vary in body condition and underlying medical problems. This is why it is essential to have regular visits with our veterinarian. However, it is extremely important to avoid obesity, particularly with us senior cats; you don't want us to walk around with pot bellies do you? The best senior diet should include high-quality protein, reduced fat, and, for energy, some carbohydrates. I'd like to also mention making sure our foods have key minerals to help support are aging joints as well as vitamins and protein, all of which will help support our aging immune system.

There are foods called "life-stage" foods that are specifically for us. These are formulated to suit us senior cats by working with our digestive system easier and helping to maintain our fine figures. The life-stage foods provide an easily-digested protein, but not all of us senior cats like them. Because they are often expensive, I would recommend that you first try getting a sample bag to see if your senior cat likes it before you buy a large amount.

When buying your cat food, I would not recommend buying or feeding your cat those "no-name" brands that are sold in pet shops, groomers, or even the Internet, not because they are usually suspiciously cheap but, primarily, because most of these are smaller companies that do not have the resources to execute quality control on their products. Additionally, smaller manufacturers differ negatively from larger ones in that their batch may be more apt to change with each one produced. Also, due to comparative popularity, cat foods of smaller companies tend to stay on the shelves longer and get stale. To be safe and beneficial for us, buy our food where you would buy your food. After all, you trust the store you go to.

Now, most veterinarians normally recommend dry cat food for all felines, but, over the years, they have noticed that felines that are on dry cat food tend to have cleaner teeth, less gum disease, and less of a problem with obesity. However, as with anything else, there is both a good side and a bad side. Veterinarians are not sure if those factors are enough to recommend a dry food diet so strongly. I myself prefer wet food over dry, but having both helps keeps my teeth clean. It is more convenient for owners to feed us dry cat food, as it is economical, but it does not meet all of your feline's nutritional needs. Ultimately, it is an unnatural diet for felines. Most dry cat foods have a much higher grain carbohydrate than cats are meant to consume – after all, our systems were not designed to be vegetarian. Furthermore, many dry cat foods are sprayed with fats that are not suitable for us, but are added anyway to make them more appealing. These fats can become rancid and unhealthy...I think I lost my appetite.

Veterinarians feel the greatest potential problem is that felines eating dry cat food exclusively almost never drink a sufficient amount of water to compensate for the deficiency in hydration. Even though such claims have not been proven, many veterinarians associate dehydration with kidney and bladder disease. Perhaps the grossest aspect of it is that dry cat foods are more susceptible to bacterial contamination (salmonella, etc.) than canned foods.

We felines do prefer the taste and smell of fish-based canned foods, but those tasty flavors get old when we have them every day, so please switch them up a little. It is true that we do love canned food more than dry. Yes, it can make us gain weight, but it is your job to keep an eye on our body weight.

Ultimately, be careful when shopping for our food. There are many products that are even marked with "Especially for Senior Cats." Every major company offers one. They are usually vague in describing what makes these foods better than the others. Most of the time, there actually is not a significant difference between their regular products and the senior products. So, please read the labels as you would for your human food.

Sometimes, although I don't really want to admit it – I do have a tendency of constipation, for which the best thing to do is to add to our food is a little extra bran fiber. We are just like you humans who have the same problem; we need our fiber too. My veterinarian recommends that we get this extra fiber over our entire life, but most owners do not know this. Of course, vitamins and minerals are particularly beneficial for our bodies, and if you buy the nationally marketed major brands of canned or dry food, we should not need any extra vitamins or minerals. However, we still benefit from receiving antioxidants once in a while such as an Omega-3 or glucosamine/chondroitin supplement. Always check with your veterinarian to make sure this is okay for us.

As we get older, we seniors do not like to swing off the drapes like we did when we were kittens; we now prefer to lay back. However, laying back too much can cause obesity, and that is not good; it transforms our fine figure into what resembles a hippo or something like that. You should have our veterinarian check us to make sure that we do not have any problems with our thyroid or have an overactive adrenal gland, which are some other factors that could cause us to lose our figure. Now, if we don't have a sluggish thyroid or an overactive adrenal gland, then it is safe to conclude that we are simply being lazy. You will have to either feed us less fattening diets, give us less of what you are currently serving to us, or increase our exercise. Well, that is what the veterinarian says, but you are not getting me on a tread mill, so you are better off just feeding me less – I do have an image to keep around this place.

Still, my veterinarian says the best way to reduce our weight is through exercise. You can purchase one of those idiotic laser pointer lights that we can't help but chase, add some cat furniture, or if your feline is an indoor cat, take them for a walk. My owner lets me out on warm, sunny days, and I walk myself around, but those that are not as fortunate as me should have their owner take them out on – God forbid – a leash. The important thing is to make sure you are getting us in shape, or feeding us the right diet to keep us healthy and fit.

The main things to remember are that we need plenty of water and both wet and dry food, and that we are not gaining way too much weight or losing too much either. Humans, please, we are not a grazing animal, so you must make sure for us that we are getting the correct food to eat. Furthermore, please help us get enough exercise, so we can keep our great, lean figures. Always keep an open door with our veterinarian so that they know how we are doing. Always listen to your feline, for we know what we need. And, of course, always give your cat lots and lots of love.

Section 2 – Grooming

Using Grooming as Bonding Time

Well, being groomed is one of my favorite pastimes with my human companion. You know cats like to groom one another, it is a way we greet each other and it is a form of us interacting with each other. But most of us felines are in our homes, and normally the only one there is our human companion and they can build a relationship with us by grooming us. This helps young and us senior cats to improve our temperaments and sociability.

Now, listen closely because I am going to give you some tips to make this enjoyable for us, as well as for you. Most of us like being stroked and enjoy the feeling of light grooming. Hey, it's in our genes, what cat doesn't like to be petted. Before I forget, one way to ease into grooming us is to massage us. Our old achy joints will benefit. When you message us, it does a couple of things; it helps loosens the stiffness, and increases circulation. Doing this will also help you and your feline to connect to each other.

Before you even reach down and grab us, approach us in a friendly way, as a senior cat we don't like to be surprised. Talk to us, and make sure you pick us up gently. Remember as we get older we are more fragile than a younger cat. When you do have us in your arms, start first by just petting us, this will relax us and calm us down, and don't forget to talk to us too.

If you need to restrain us, please remember to do this gently, especially with us senior cats. If you see us starting to panic, let us go and don't force us to sit still or in some awkward position for too long also. Be careful when grooming and not being too exuberant. How would you like having your hair pulled out, it hurt us too, and even more because it is our whole body that is full of hair.

Also, know when to stop. You might not be able to groom us all in one session and that is okay. Give us a break and come back in a day or two and finish up. Remember it is better to have a good time making us happy, than giving us a bad time where we will not let you touch us.

Now as a senior cat, we need to be groomed more often, and well, especially around the anal area. We are getting old and it is hard for us to keep our behinds clean, so we do need help. Remember, the more grooming you do to us; it helps us to keep down on hairballs and other problems.

Remember to make this grooming time a happy bonding time between you and you senior cat. I love my time with my human when they groom me. Well, below I am going to mention some things you should know about grooming and how it should be done properly so that you and your senior cat will enjoy your time together.

Remember it is important to groom us because it is a part of keeping us healthy through our lives, even when we do get old. As your feline gets older, you humans have to take a more active role in grooming us. We senior cats often groom less, and we do have trouble cleaning some of those "hard to reach places," like behind our ears, and even near a behinds. If these areas are not clean they can develop in a skin condition. So don't forget you will need to keep an active part in keeping your cat clean and monitoring any changes in our skin or coat.

Grooming as a Health Check

Once you have us in your lap, and making us feel calm and relax, start to feel our bodies for lumps and bumps. These lumps could be within the surface of the skin. Always have your veterinarian evaluate any new skin growths. These lumps or bumps can sometimes be a nuisance to us, and sometimes if they are located in sensitive areas, they are just right out aggravating. Also make sure when you are grooming that you are very careful to not rip them open and make them bleed. The best thing to do if you feel these lumps or bumps is to have them checked out. They could just be something not to worry about or something to be worry about like a tumor.

We also get these lumps or bumps in areas that we lost muscle mass, like by our knees and hip joints. If you see these areas having them, then you need to make sure we have a comfortable place for us to rest. As we get older we cannot sleep on hard surfaces, it is just not good for us, how would you like at 98 years old to sleep on a hard, cold floor. That's what I thought, we don't like it either.

So while petting us and even before you bring out the brushes, check us over to make sure that you don't feel any lumps or bumps. This will make us both very happy if you do this, I personally don't like pain when something such as grooming is to make us feel good. So do your senior cat a favor and check them over before starting any grooming.

You should also be checking out our skin to see if it is dry and flaking, if it is, it could be because we are having trouble spreading oils within our bodies. The normal way us felines do this is by licking ourselves, this is how we spread the oils throughout our skin and fur, which is how we get a shiny and smooth coat. So what do you do if you notice this, when grooming us regularly helps to spread a natural oil we have over our coats keeping them shinny and healthy. This oil is in our sebaceous glad, which is like the Omega-3 oil. It is important that you give us this Omega-3 in our diets. If you don't want to give us the Omega-3 then you should feed us more fish, like tuna, that's what I am talking about. This Omega-3 is great for our skin and fur. It is our fountain of youth.

We too get gray hair, and it is more noticed on black cats. If our hair becomes thinner and dull, it could be more than we just need Omega-3 in our diets, you should have your veterinarian check to make sure that we are aging gracefully.

Just like our human companions we too get arthritis which makes it hard for us to reach certain places. Also as we age our mental stage also changes, which can give us lack of interest in grooming ourselves. As with any senior we may need help by more frequent brushings, bathing's or medicated shampoos.

If you notice that we are shedding a lot, this is also because as we get older we cannot take care of ourselves as we use to. So to minimize this, you can use a wired slicker cat brush for long hair, or bristled brush for short haired cats, and gently brushing in the direction your cat hair flows, this will remove the loose hairs.

My veterinarian mentioned that there is a disease of the endocrine system that causes our skin to change. If our hormonal becomes imbalance, it will make our skin fragile by making it thin. It can also make it tear easily and make us heal slower too. So if you see any changes in appearance, color or order of the skin you should have our veterinarian check us out.

Well, I think you are ready to learn what makes a great relationship with us; it is all in the grooming. Below I will tell you the basics and proper why to groom your senior cat without you getting clawed to death. By the way, you might want to make sure that our claws are trimmed before started, just in case.

Brushing

Well, as we get old, there are many reasons that we might not be able to clean ourselves. As we get older we are not as energized and we start to get lazy and gain weight, but I would have to say that the most common reason is due to orthopedic problems, arthritis, just as our human friends as they get older.

When you brush us, you are removing dead hairs from our coats, this helps us to not get matted fur, and of course less hair balls. Brushing helps to stimulate blood circulation and the sebaceous-gland in the skin, which makes our coat healthier.

So you will need some basic equipment to make sure we are being groomed properly.

Basic equipment you need for grooming your cat

When buying your bushes you need to make sure to buy those that are soft with plastic tip type teeth. The metals ones hurt our skin, making us not want to be groomed. We don't like the metal type of brushes and combs due that one they are very hard and normally sharp. If you start pulling my hair, it also starts to hurt my skin more too. There are times that you will have to use a wire type brush or a metal comb if my hair is matted and it also help to pick up excess dander. But please try to get the brushes that are comfortable to my skin. How would you like a brush that feels more like a rake scraping your scalp?

If you do buy a metal comb, make sure that it is s sturdy stainless-steel comb with a wide-set of teeth and that they are rounded on the tips. You will need also a slicker brush that has bristles, it looks like a tiny bent nails. Remember, please if you use these metal type combs and brushes, do so with care on my skin.

Another type of comb you will want to buy is a flea comb. These are a metal combs' that their teeth are very close to each other. This comb will help to remove fleas and their eggs. The brush is also good as a touch-up comb after using the slicker brush.

Grooming mitts are also good to brush us, because they fit over your whole hand, and it lets you work fast on brushing your whole cat quickly.

Basic brushing techniques on seniors

Brushing is important to help remove dead hair and to help to keep the hairballs down. It also helps us to have a shiny coat and gives us a good feeling inside. We normally spend about a third of our waking time grooming, but as we get older that becomes less, so it helps when our human friends help us in this area. Please remember as you brush our skin becomes more sensitive as we get older so please take care when brushing.

We should be brushed or combed daily, helps to keep the loose hair to a minimal, and to help us from not swallowing hair balls. Daily brushing can be very relaxing and enjoyed as a quality time for me and my owner.

When you decided to start to groom us, you should choose a time that I am relaxed and not feeling hyper, of course as we get older, we don't normally feel too hyper. But this will help to make sure things go a lot easier.

When starting to groom, you should first brush against the growth of the hair. This helps to get all of the loose hair that is between the layers of hair, so groom with the growth of the hair, this helps to make sure you are getting whatever is left on top. Make sure you are brushing me everywhere too.

Don't forget my head, back, tail, stomach and legs. Once you are done using the brush, you can use a metal comb to remove dead fleas if there are any. By grooming us on a regular basis, will also keep you aware if we are getting any fleas or tick on us, which means it is time for that flea powder.

Please, once you are done brushing your cat, remove the hair from the comb or brush before using it again, and if you are planning to use it on another cat, you might want to wash it thoroughly too. If your cat has a skin disorder, don't use the same equipment on another cat, use another brush and comb so you are not spreading the disorder to another cat. Your cat will thank you for that.

Once you are done brushing, rub us down with a soft cloth in order to catch any loose hair to prevent him from getting hair balls when he licks himself. You could even dampen the cloth very little, to get all the hair, plus it feels like another cat's licking us then too.

Of course depending on your cat, each cat sheds differently. An outdoor cat sheds more in the spring and fall time, and indoor cats tend to shed all year long. The type of brush or comb will depend on your cats hair also. Short hair, you would use a shorter metal comb or brush, and of course with a long hair, you will need a longer one. If you cat is a long hair, you will need to brush them daily to prevent matting.

One of the areas that as we get older is hard for us, well it is our behinds. Once you are done brushing us, you will need to use a damp tissue or pet wipes and gentle wipe us. This is important because, if not cleaned, it will start to clump and matt, then there is the odor, and it also could cause raw spots on my skin. So please keep this area clean for your senior cats.

If the butt area is bad, you might have to shave the hair. You can do a couple of things. You can wash the area to soften and maybe get most of the matter and clumps out. You can use scissors to cut away the hair, but the fastest is to shave the area. Once the area is shaved or cleared away, make sure that there is no raw spots, if there is please take us to the vet for medication. As we are older, you need make sure that are behinds are well kept clean, and make sure there is not much hair there. This will help to keep the area easier to manage.

Preventing Hairballs

Well, just in case you don't know what a hairball is, it is hair, duh! We get them when we clean ourselves, our tongues grab the hair and we swallow. As we swallow the hair it starts to build up forming a hairball. Hair does not digest in our stomach, and we have trouble pass hair though our digestive system. So the only way we can get rid of this hairball is by coughing them up most of the time, but sometimes this is quite hard to do when you are old. If we consume too much, it can cause intestinal blockage and constipation. Now listen to me closely, we seniors cannot handle hairballs as when we were younger.

Grooming is the main thing you can really help us in keeping the hairballs down. There is some companies that make food for us that have additives, that help us to pass hairballs, there is also pet grass that we can eat that can help. But grooming is the main thing that can help the most by reducing the loose hair.

Although in the worst case, if your cat swallows so much hair and cannot pass it at all, you must take them to your veterinarian right away, surgery may be needed to save their lives. But for the most part, hairballs don't usually cause these types of problems if you feed them with special foods that can help and lots of grooming.

There are some simple steps that you can take to help keep the hairballs under control. Brush your cat regularly. This will help keep the loose hairs, and keeping less out of your cats' stomach. Find a dry cat food that has hairball control, these are normally right on the label, and they contain more fiber to help pass hairballs if swallowed. There are also cat treats that have hairball control also, that too can help, and your cat will love you for those too. One of the worst things that cause hairballs is having a feline that has long hair, you might have to keep it trimmed to help keep down the hairballs. For a last resort, you can put some petroleum jelly on your cats' paws or nose and your cat will lick it up, helping it to pass hairballs. Just make sure that the petroleum jelly is not having any added ingredients or fragrance, just use the plain kind.

Getting knots and Matted hair out

Matted hair is when our hair gets knotted up, especially in areas that we sit or lay on the most. This could be on our bellies, and as we get older, more toward our behind, and beneath our necks. These hurt as they keep matting. It is like for your humans, that if I took your hair and kept twisting it, and twisting it, it will start to pull your skin and hurt. That is how it feels for us too.

There is a mat breaker comb that works great for this and you may find that it is quicker than having your love one under anesthetic. Remember most of the matting areas for us old cats are because we cannot reach those areas anymore.

When starting to remove matted hair, please be very gentle. If you start to come in like you are going to saw at it, you might find us clawing you, and trying to get out of there. Start by gently using the metal comb to gently pull the mats out. You can continue this until you are finished, and you can gently take the comb through without snagging. An important thing here to note is, to do small areas at a time.

If you groom us on a regular basis, we should not have many problems with matting. But if your cat does get matted hair so bad that it is hard for you to get a comb through, then you can do two things. You can either trim your cat with electric or scissors yourself, or take it in to a professional.

Normally I would not want my hair trimmed due that it can get cold, but I rather be cold than having my skin getting pulled out from the twisting. My owner does a great job at using electric trimmers and she makes it look easy too. If you cannot get them out by a comb, use the trimmers, this would need two people though. If you never have trimmed your cats hair before, below is a way for you to do this.

Trimming Your Cat's Hair

My owner puts me on her lap and places in a way that I am pinned in. Now for some cats, they might need to be held while someone else does the trimming. But the main thing is to make sure you keep talking to us, and make sure your trimmers are for animals. These types of trimmers normally are a lot quieter than the ones you humans use.

Now when trimming the hair, you have to go in the same direction that the hair grows. This is to prevent nicking our skin and cutting us. If you are trimming around our behinds, this is an area when we get old is the hardest for us to keep clean. When we use the bathroom, our feces often get tangled in our hair and also can cause matting. This area should be trimmed on a regular basis for us seniors, believe me, we would very much appreciate it. If there is a lot to do, do it in short turns, giving us a break as well as you.

The main thing is to take it slow, and always talk to us.

Nails

The basic tools for your cat's nails

One of the things that we do not like the most is having our nails trimmed. So before you grab us and start clipping away please be gentle with us. You should play with your cat's paws and toes for fun sometimes, this could help us not to associate every time you come to us that you are going to clip our nails. You can invest is a specialized cat clippers which is recommended, or you can just use an ordinary human clippers.

Basic care before you start trimming

We senior cats do not wear down our claws as quickly as we did when we were younger, so because they grow in a curved manner, they start curl into our paws. This hurts more than you having a hang nail, try walking on your own nails. Normally as we get older, our nails get more brittle, so they are more likely to break off but the nail sheaths may not let it as easily as when I might use the scratching post. As we get older we do not use the scratching post as much as we like due to arthritis, or just because of our reduced general activity. So we need you to take care of our nails to make sure they are trimmed nicely.

Most senior cats will need their nails clipped often and especially if your cat is an indoor cat. They should be checked on a weekly basis and trim if necessary. Overgrown nails get us snagged on carpets, furnishings and even your nice shirts when we cuddle up to you. Also when we pull away, our nails can get snagged, and cause injury to me when pulling free.

Now it doesn't have to be an ordeal thing if you are gentle with us and are careful when clipping. You should always make sure to make it fun and playful; this will help keep the stress down.

How to trim the nails correctly and safely

To start, pick up gently and put us on a table holding us from behind, keeping our backs close to your stomach. This helps us not to be scared of the nail clippers, and if we do try to step back we are not going away.

Gently grab our paw and start by rubbing them gently, and then gently press on the top. This will cause our toes to spread and our nails to become exposed. Check to see if they are sharp and pointy, if they are then we need them clipped.

You can clip with professional clippers which are the best to make sure you are trimming them correctly, but you can also use human clippers. The problem using human clippers is that you can't get a good trim from top to bottom.

Now if you see that they do need to be clipped, make sure you hold the clippers the right way. Most people want to clip at right angles to the nail, cutting across the nail. This is not good; it makes our nails more subject to splitting or fraying. Now pay attention, when using clippers hold them in a position where you can clip from the bottom to the top, I do not want to lose my nails or get hurt. Remember when you are clipping, you only want to get rid of the sharp point. Always try to stay away from the pink tissue ("quick"), this is the nails blood supply and if you do cut into this, it really hurts, and you might find yourself scratched up as well.

We also have a thumb nail, which is further up our leg. These tend to overgrow more than our main nails. So remember to check these as well.

What do you do if you accidentally clip into the pink tissue ("quick"), well stay calm. The claw will bleed for a moment, but it will usually stop very quickly. Keep us calm by talking to us and patting us. If the bleeding doesn't stop, you can use a styptic pencil to the claw end or styptic powder. Just remember to always keep us calm if you want us to return to you.

Well you have it, just remember to do each toe. The more you do it, you senior cat will not mind the help. If you do have a senior cat that has long hair, you might need an extra hand to help move the hair away from the paws.

You should check on our nails every ten to fourteen days to make sure they stay nice and trimmed. If you keep your senior cat calm, it can be an enjoy time together, but if your cat doesn't like his nails touch at all, then to save you from becoming a pin cushion, then you should have a professional do it, or even your veterinarian.

Bathing

Being a senior cat, I can tell you now that I personally don't like baths, and really don't need one. There are some cats that might need to have a bath because they smell or got into things. Another reason senior cats might need to be wash is if they have fleas or a skin allergy. When bathing your senior cats, you really should try to see other ways first; baths can be very traumatizing to us.

Using the right shampoo

Always make sure that you use the right shampoo. Please do not use human shampoo, because they do not have the right pH balance, and can hurt our skin. If you must use human shampoo for heaven sakes, make sure that is a baby shampoo. But the best thing to do is to go to your pet store and buy shampoo for cats. If you are buying flea shampoo, this can be very toxic to us and should be very careful when using. Make sure to always read the label on the back of the shampoo for the best use on your cat.

Basic Things you Need

Things that you should have ready before giving your cat a bath. Make sure you have the right shampoo that is for cats anything else could be hard on our skin. Put all the items you need by the sink that you are going to bath your cat in. You should have at least two towels, the shampoo, and my human likes to use this measuring cup that is filled up with eight cups of warm water. A small soft bristle toothbrush to clean our face and ears.

Bathing

The first thing that I want to mention is again, if you feel you just need to wash your senior cat to just clean them, then just use a warm wash cloth that is semi damp and wipe them down with this. It is less stressful and still can get the job done. But if you have to do deep cleaning and there is no other way, than a bath is what you must do.

How to Bath your Senior

Before washing your senior, try to as much to brush them and get all the matted hair out and anything else that might be stuck in the hair. I am sorry to say as I am getting older, it is hard to clean the back end, and sometimes debris will get stuck, and even feces will dry and stay attached. The sink that you are going to wash your senior in, should be deep enough that you can keep control of us, but hard for us to get out. Fill the sink or tub with only enough warm water that is needed to wash us. You might want to wear an apron when doing this too. Also, I recommend doing this in a room where you can close the door, so that we cannot get out of the room, when we try.

When starting to wash your senior, hold us with our stomach resting on your forearm. This give you a better control and it also lets us know that you are in control. Start by getting us wet with the other hand, and then about a dime size of shampoo in your hand, start to lather all over. If you have to wash areas that have dried feces, first use a damp warm washcloth with some mild soap. One, this will soften up the dried feces, then use a brush to brush the hairs. If there is still some feces, then wash again. Please be careful behind there, we seniors do not like all that pulling, how would you like if someone is pulling hair out of your behind. Once you have the shampoo on me, leave on for a few minutes, about five minutes, this will kill the fleas and to make sure we are clean. Then with your warm cup of water, start to rinse us off. Make sure you rinse us off very well; the dry soap can make us itch or get a rash. To wash around the face, you should use a wash cloth or a soft bristle toothbrush, and gently wash these areas, making sure you do not get soap into our eyes. When washing the face, you could put cotton in our ears to make sure you don't get water in them. Once you are done, grab a towel and start to dry us off, and you don't need to rub us to hard either. As you are drying us off, you should be brushing us to make sure we are clean, and no hair is loose. Plus it makes us look great.

My human says that the trick in bathing us is to be as gentle as possible and to get us out of the bath quickly, this minimizes any trauma. If your cat is an indoor cat, you can let him go loose in the house. If your senior cat stays outside most of the time, then make sure they are completely dried before letting out, especially in cooler weather.

Ears

We like are ears rubbed, and they are very important to us, so you need to look at our ears carefully. Please do not just grab our ears like is it some silly putty either, be gentle when you look and care for our ears. Doing regular checks of our ears is an important part of our health care. It is a good idea to do a weekly check to be able to prevent any problems. It is easy for us, and especially for us older seniors to get things like ear mites, yeast infection, a bacterial infection and even fungal infection that is on the tip of our ears.

Did you know that when I was younger, just a young kitten we can hear a bag a treats, or even a can of food being open from another part of the house. We can pick up sounds at 50 to 60 kilohertz, compare to what you humans can. I think humans pick up something like 16 to 20 kilohertz. Of course as we get older we are no different than our human companions, we can slowly lose our hearing.

Examine the Ear
The first thing that my human companion does is check my outer ear. On our ear, we have what is called a pinna, it has a layer of hair on the outside of it. These should be clean and have a light pink color to it; this is a way to tell that we are a health cat. If for any reasons you see redness or even discharge coming from that area, please take us to the veterinarian. Once you examine the outside of the ear, then it is time to examine the inner ear. Please, for Cat Sake, do not stick a Q-Tip in the canal of the ear. My human normally would check my ears while I let them sit by me. You want to check for a health pink color, and no debris or bad odors. If

we have way too must wax or a bad odor, you will want to take us to the veterinarian to have our ears examined.

Now, I do not mind my human cleaning my ears, and if you are going to clean our senior cat's ears, you will need some equipment. You will need your ear wash solution, some cotton balls, and some tweezers to pluck hair. If you are going to use Q-Tips, just do not go down in the canal. My human uses olive oil, and warm water to clean out my ears.

Cleaning the Ear
The best way to clean your senior ears out, you should first place a drop or two of your cleaning solution into the ear canal. Now, please just do not leave that in our ears, massage the base of the ear for about a minute or two so that the liquid gets around and softens whatever may need to be clean. This should be done at about four or five times in each ear. Once both ears are done, leave your cat alone for a moment, and let them shake their heads, this will help to dislodge any dirt and move it into the outer ear canal. After about five minutes, my human then takes clean cotton balls to wipe away any of the olive oil and dirt in the ear. Make sure you clean everything up well, and then give us a treat for being such a good cat, I like cheese, even if it does give me gas.

You can buy special ear cleaning solutions for feline at pet stores like PetCo, or PetsSmart, and you should be able find some on Amazon as well. My human likes to use natural products like olive oil, some even use vinegar, just make sure that it is safe for your feline.

Infected Ears

My human and I wanted to put a list of things that you should look for, to help guide you in knowing what is an infected ear. There are ways to tell when we have an infected ear; there could be redness in the ear, a discharge or a bad odor. Or if you see us shaking our heads a lot, and no it does not mean we are say no, or going crazy. If you see us scratching our ears a lot could also be a sign of an infection. The main thing to remember that a good air flow is important for us to maintain a healthy ear.

There will be times when you will have to take us to the veterinarian to have our ears check more thoroughly when there are signs of an infection. So it is a good idea in knowing some of the ear disorders that your feline can get.

Ear mites, these are parasites that look like coffee grounds, and they are very contagious to your other pets. Most ear infections are normally caused by bacteria, a yeast infection or a foreign debris caught in the ear canal. These are more serious and we should be taken to a vet immediately. Blood blisters are a caused by blood accumulation in our ear flap. These are often caused by ear mites, fleas or trapped debris.

Ear hematoma is a more collection of clotted blood from broken blood vessels on the ear flap. When the cat either scratches or shakes their head, this will rupture the blood vessel. You should take us to the veterinarian if you see this.

Otitis external is another inflammation of the outer ear. These are mostly caused by either bacteria or a yeast infection.

Sunburn for feline that have white hair or very little on their heads, noses and ears. For some reason more humans do not think about how we too can get burned by the big bright light in the sky. If there is not enough shade for us to sit, then there should be some made, or do not let us stay out too long. Also what goes with sunburn is Squamous cell carcinoma; again it is an excessive exposure to sunlight and seen more in white cat. This is also more common in older outdoor cats than a younger cat.

Frostbite is another serious one; we live in a cold state that winter can get way below zero. Our ears are very vulnerable because they are more exposed than any other parts of our bodies. If you see any discoloration, redness or even blackening you need to get us warmed up, and might need to take us to the veterinarian.

So it is very important for you to keep a good eye on our ears, we need them to scout for those mice when we are in the mood.

Eyes

Look into my eyes, and you will see one smart senior cat. I want to squash a bad superstition that cats are color blind. Well we are not, we can see some color, and we can also get cataracts and have other eye problems just like our human companions. My eyes are just as important as yours, and need to be looked at regularly to make sure they stay that way.

Washing the Eye

When you groom your senior cat, look into their great eyes, and they should be clear and bright. We have a tendency sometimes of having runny or weepy tears that flow from the tear ducts. If these tears are left to turn into crust, it may cause to block our tear ducts, and get infected. Here is an idea that my human companion does. Take distilled water and boil it, and while it is boiling, add a teaspoon of table salt. Make sure that all the salt is dissolved before letting the water cool down to room temperature. Take a nice soft washcloth and dip it into the water, wring the washcloth out, and gently wipe the eyes.

If you put us into a large bath towel, this will help you to hold us better, and maybe we won't have you for lunch. The towel will serve as a protection for you and a better hold. Just make sure you swaddle us in the towel, and make sure we are in a natural and comfortable position, if not then you will need to be ready for a fight.

You might want to use cotton balls to do each eye, then when you get all the crusted off, then take your washcloth and do a nice gentle rub. Just make sure that you do one eye at a time, so that you do not cross infect the other eye if there is an infection. This is why cotton balls are better to use first on each eye.

Checking our Eyes

Humans should be checking our eyes every day or every other day to make sure that our eyes stay healthy and bright. When grooming your senior cat, you should always over look us to make sure we are healthy, and check to make sure our eyes are not swollen or appear red. If you see these things, or even discharge that you will need to make sure you clean them right away, and then contact the veterinarian.

Did you know that we too can catch feline conjunctivitis, which is a feline pink eye. It can be caught by humans, but it is very rare. Another thing that you should look at is our third eyelid; this is that white eyelid that is under our upper and lower eyelids. If you see me squinting, or that this third eyelid is showing a lot, this could be a serious eye problem that our veterinarian will need to be contacted.

If your senior cat has long hair, you should try to trim this hair away from the eyes. This long hair can also scratch the eye and cause infection. Remember that the health of your senior cat is very important for them to see. As we get older it gets hard enough to get around, and we need our eyes to see. Oh, yeah, if you have to give your senior cat any type of eye drop medication, it works best to tilt our head back, and gently put in your one or two drops as prescribed. If for some reason that you need to put more than one medication in the eye, it would be best to wait about 10 minutes between treatments, otherwise you will have a serious upset senior. I also recommend having at least two human companions in doing this. It will help one to hold; well the other puts the drops in.

Another important thing to watch is to make sure we don't grow a third eye, in the middle of our heads, just kidding, making sure you are paying attention.

Cleaning the Teeth

We too are like humans in keeping our teeth clean. Especially senior cats, were we do not eat as many things as we did when we were young kittens. But, I will have to tell you I do not like something in my mouth or down my throat. That is just me of course. Well, I should at least tell you how important it is, so that you're senior cat will stay healthy.

There is special tooth paste that is sold to clean our teeth. I do not know how it tastes because again, I am one that does not like fingers in my mouth. This toothpaste can be bought at most pet stores, and should really be done.

The best way to clean your senior cats' teeth is by first getting them use to the taste of the paste, and rewarding them as they are doing this. You can start by putting some on your finger and rub them on the tooth. One idea is and that is because I love tuna, is to dip your finger in tuna water and let your senior cat lick your fingers. After a couple of session then put some tuna water onto a gauze and rub this on your seniors tooth. They will love the taste of the tuna, and when you start to switch from tuna to the toothpaste, they would not mind. Make sure you give them treats too, we love our treats.

The toothpaste has flavors that your feline will like, and this will make brushing their teeth easier. Make sure you keep praising your cat, and talking to them. We like when our humans companions talk to us. Make sure you brush the upper canine teeth; those are the nice long ones that we love to chow down with. As your senior cat gets uses to having these two canine teeth done, start doing more of the teeth, and always give praises and treats.

Having the teeth done is very important and should be at least twice a week, and you should start this practice when your cats are young so that they are used to having this done. But seniors will need it done to stay healthy. Just be careful not to get bit if your senior is cranky.

Nose

We senior cats are no different than our human companions; we too get the common cold. When you see us having a stuffy nose, which would be the main reason, the common cold. It is a good idea to keep our nose clean so that we do not get an infection. We cannot blow our nose like our humans companions can.

The best way to clean our nose is with a warm and moist washcloth. Just make sure you clean our noses well so that it will not dry up and become crusty. Our noses also can become dry and start to get chapped, to resolve this; you can use petroleum jelly, but please only a small dab, not a glob. Repeat this at least twice a day until we are no longer stuffy and our little noses are no longer chapped.

If our stuffiness is really bad, put us in a room that is humid to help break up our stuffy noses. If you have one of those humidifier, that would work too if you place it the same room that I sleep at. My human companion puts me in the bath room that has been steamed by the shower. I love this, because is nice and warm, and I just take another nap till they open the door.

When using a tissue to wipe our nose, please make sure it is the soft stuff. Please do not use the tissues that you would not even use on your nose, those hurt. Better yet, use cotton balls instead of tissues, they are softer and small enough to handle. Also, please do not use the same tissue on our eyes, throw those away, and take a clean one, which is why using a cotton ball is better. Clean the nose, and throw it away. Grab another and wipe our eyes, then through that one away. You get the point, I hope so.

If there seems to be more than a couple days that go by, you should take us to our veterinarian, just in case it is nothing more than a common cold. Remember, also as we become seniors, we are thinner and just like human seniors, we cannot take cold weather well. So do not leave us out side to the point where I have to yell by the door to let me in. By that time, I am already too cold, and it will make me sick. How would you like if I left your grandma outside till she was at the door yelling to come in.

Again, by doing a daily patting, you should always keep a good eye on our health.

When is a Professional Groomer Needed?

I left this for last because, most human companions of felines will want to take care of their own cats, and it is something that will help them bond with their seniors. It's like visiting you grandparents, you do it because you love them and want to keep that bond.

I believe that one would need a professional groomer if your cat is a fighter, which at my age, I can only yell, I do not have the energy to do more than that. Another reason that you might want to see a professional would be if your cat needs a bath, and you really cannot do it. This could be safer for you and your feline. Having a longhair cat, you might need a professional. They get knotted up easy, and long hair is hard to maintain.

Make sure you find a good cat groomer, and that they specialize in cats. Dog groomers are not cat groomers. Most dog groomers might do a cat once in a while; you do not want those types. There are groomers that mainly do cats. They are trained and skilled to handle cats.

Section 3 – Exercising

Have you ever watched those "Jane Fanda" workout videos? I remember my human companion watching those or even those "Rich Simmons, Sweat with the oldies". Well, keep watching them, because you are not going to get my old bones to do those kinds of things. Can you picture this 98 year old, 20 in human years, wearing a sweat outfit and doing Sweat with the oldies, ha, ha. Exercise is important for any cat, and especially one that is older to keep fit. As we get older we lose a lot of fat and muscle tissue. If we did exercise more, this would slow the aging process down some.

Exercising is important for our health, and for our circulatory. It helps us to keep our muscles and to not gain weight. Most veterinarian suggest about 10 minutes a day and at least twice a day. Exercising can be either done by taking us for a walk if your feline is not an outdoor cat, and to play with us.

Exercising

We are a predator type animal, so we like to play that gives us the feel of hunting. We like those toys that look and smell like mice, birds and even bugs. I heard my veterinarian talk about special videos that you can buy and it will get us into the mood. That would be interesting, running up to some screen and smashing my face, well not for me. These videos could be for others cats though, and you might want to look into it.

Having Play Time

Make sure that you are making time to have play time with your senior. If they are mainly an indoor cat, then this is even more important. Most senior cats are already at the age that we do not want to do much, and if we are left alone all day in the home, we become lazier. This is way it is important to spend at least 10 to 15 minutes a day to play.

Toys

There are a lot of toys that are out there, I prefer a real mouse myself, or that bird that keeps bothering me when I am sleeping. But there are things that have feathers, strings, fluffy toys and many others. There is this great stuff that smells good too, I think I heard my human companion call it, "catnip". That stuff is great; it makes you feel like you can fly. There are toys that are made that this catnip is inside of them, these are the best. Take some of the toys that do have catnip in them and hide them under carpets, or blankets, and as the day go by, it gives us something to look for and have fun with.

There are also high tech type toys, but this does not always mean they are good. The one that I love playing with my human companions is the one with a red light. I love chasing that all over. Word of advice, make sure that we can at lease catch it once in a while otherwise we will lose interest. I like how my companion makes it disappear behind doors and couches. There are others that are coming out, but not sure how good they are.

A low tech toy is a rolled up paper, I love hitting that thing around the house like a mouse. Oh, yea I also love an open bag on the floor, and crawling into them, so much fun. One should also have a climbing post so we can climb and lay on a flat part, or climb into and sleep. Make sure they are good for scratching on too. We like trees, and these indoor trees are nice.

The point is that each day twice a day, you should make sure our minds are being stimulated and our bodies are being exercised to keep us fit.

Safety

There are some things that you should be aware of. First if you see us starting to have a hard time breathing, or getting tired very quickly, this could be a disease and should be checked out. With toys that have strings, feathers basically anything that we can swallow, should not be left out alone with us. We will want to play with it when you are not home, and could choke on them. So it is better that these are put away when you are not home. Last thing; change up on the toys that you do play with us so that we do not get bored.

Well, enough talk, it has been a long day and it is time for my 4 O'Clock nap time.

Conclusion

I hope that this book was able to help you with your elderly cat. Our four legged family members are so dear to us that as they age, we need to make sure we cater to them even more. By using this book, I hope that it will help in some if not all areas in taking care of your elderly cat. Elderly cat care is different than just taking care of a cat; they have special needs, just as an elderly human. With the right care, it will help our four legged family members to live a little longer, and be in the best shape that they can be.

A Thank you

I really hope you enjoyed reading this book. If so, please leave our author a good rating and a great review. You are an integral part of our continued success. Please also share with your friends on Facebook and Twitter. Our number one goal is to help our four legged family members.

If you would like to see other things added to this book for future editions, please contact Tomsyn through **jittreasures@gmail.com**.

Preview of Next Book in the Series – Vol. 2

Cleaning Cat Messes – Cleaning Those Tough Cat Stains – From the View of a Cat is written specifically for cat lovers who have to clean up after them.

The target audience for this book is those who have cats, and know that our love ones will make messes. This is a great guide for those who need help in cleaning those messes up, and getting rid of that nasty order that these messes can leave. This guide will even show how to get rid of those older stains that are left behind over the years.

This book was written in a unique way, that it was told through the eyes of a cat. This makes learning of how to clean these messes in a funnier way from the view of my cat, Mama Kitty.

By learning how to clean these messes, it will help to keep your house smelling clean and free from bad orders that cats do leave behind. Having a clean house is great for you and your cat.

When we chose to bring that special cat into our lives, they become a part of our family. We owe them the best lives that we can give them. We owe them the best care when we get them as kittens, and as they age. As a cat owner, it is our job to clean up after our four legged family member when they do make a mess. This book will help you learn new ways in cleaning new and old messes.

Soon will be available.

Preview of Third Book in the Series – Vol. 3

What is My Cat Saying – Knowing What Your Cat is Trying to Tell You – From the View of a Cat is written specifically for those cat lovers who want to understand their four-legged family member better.

This book is to help you understand your feline a little better. What makes this book funny is that it is told by a young cat named Mr. Thomas. The things that he will be talking about are so secretive that other cats do not want you to know.

Did you ever wonder what your cat is saying when they meow to you. What about when your cat holds their tail up in the air or swishes it back and forth. Do not forget about the ears too. Your cats' body language is just like the human body language where once you learn some of the basics, you will be able to understand better your four-legged family members better.

What is My Cat Saying – Knowing What Your Cat is Trying to Tell You – From the View of a Cat came about when owners started to wonder, why is my little boy, or girl meowing off the top of their lungs, or they sound so sad. What does it mean when they purr or wink at me? What does it mean when they bring me a dead mouse? These and more questions will be answered by Mr. Thomas telling you more from his view of why he does what he does.

This book is diffidently a great read, and informative if you are a cat, lover.

Soon will be available.

Other Books by J I & T Treasures

Cat Series by Tomsyn

Senior Cat Care – How to Take Care of Your Elderly Cat – From the View of a Cat – Vol. 1

(Now available)

Cleaning Cat Messes – Cleaning Those Tough Cat Stains – From the View of a Cat – Vol. 2

(Soon will be available)

What is My Cat Saying – Knowing What Your Cat is Trying to Tell You – From the View of a Cat – Vol. 3

(Soon will be available)

Made in the USA
Las Vegas, NV
03 January 2024

83779041R10046